TURN ON YOUR LIGHT

FINDING YOUR LIGHT WITHIN

Share your light!
—SENECA

SENECA WILSON

Seneca Wilson Group Publishing
For more information visit: www.senecawilson.com

Book cover: David Anderson
Edited by Matt Toomey
Interior layout: OA.Blueprints, LLC.

Turn On Your Light/ Seneca Wilson. -- 1st ed. ISBN 978-0-578-75853-4

Also by Seneca Wilson | Stairs to the Top & Kind of a One

Praise for
Turn on Your Light
by Seneca Wilson

Seneca's story is one of perseverance, determination, and personal growth. He transformed his life through the power of education and his commitment to accepting effective mentoring. Seneca's light shines bright today as he inspires others through interpersonal relationships, poetry, spoken word, and now by revealing his compelling and authentic story. *- Stan L. Shingles, Vice President, Central Michigan University*

Turn on Your Light: Finding Your Light Within is not one of those books that tells you how to think. Rather, it approaches you from the perspective that we all have potential if we see it and are willing to pull it out of ourselves. Reading the book is like sitting down with a family elder who shares the stories of how he gained wisdom and purpose in his life. It makes you think. It will make it easier to find your personal wisdom and purpose. *- Paul Brailsford, CEO, Brailsford & Dunlavey, Centers, LLC*

Life continues to teach us that your past does not dictate your future. Our parents teach us that we are the masters of our own fate and with hard work, dedication, and will power we can control our own destiny. However, life also teaches us that not every person is dealt the same deck of cards or gets the same opportunities. To a Black man in America, life teaches lessons of a dark past but Seneca's message is one of hope and the promise of a brighter future. Seneca's story teaches us to dream big and dare to be extraordinary. This is his story and it's only the beginning. *- Rep. Jeramey Anderson, Mississippi House of Representatives, District 110*

I have had the privilege to watch Seneca Wilson's growth as a black man since his time as an undergraduate student at the University of Southern Mississippi. My first memories of a young brother searching to find his way have morphed into my view of what he has become, an impressive man that now fills me with a sense of pride while at the same time providing a constant source of inspiration. Not only did he figure out how to turn on his light, but the glow from that light helps others to find the switch to turn on their own lights. Seneca is a truly gifted person who has much to offer through his words, whether spoken or written. *- Dr. Kevin Marbury, Vice President, University of Oregon*

It seems like just yesterday when I watched Seneca and his sister Trina walk from their back door to this "new beacon of hope," the Boys & Girls Clubs of Jackson County's Summer Camp in Charles Warner Housing Project. He was shy, soft spoken and eager to get along with everyone. Seneca came from a humble beginning and overcame many challenges and obstacles to become the man he is today. He is a dedicated and loving husband, father, son, brother, uncle and friend. His love and respect for life can be seen through his work and his ability to reach his full potential as a productive, caring, responsible citizen.

The Boys & Girls Club made such a positive impact on Seneca's life that his mother had to visit the club to see who these people were that her son talked about all the time. The club consisted of an army of dedicated and caring staff, a safe environment, high-quality programs and unique experiences. The club was a second home for Seneca in which his dreams and aspirations were "fed". Seneca Wilson's journey began in June 1992, when his light was turned on at the Boys & Girls Clubs of Jackson County. In this book, Seneca shares how feeding positive dreams and aspirations can prove to be beneficial along life's journey. *- Catherine Glaude, Chief Executive Officer, Boys & Girls Clubs of Jackson County*

iv

DEDICATION

This book is dedicated to my wife, Meghan and children, Tylan, Declan, and Sloane. I am blessed to have you all in my life. You give me the power and strength to continue to turn on and shine my light on the world. I love you all.

Table of Contents

Acknowledgements

This work was possible because of the special individuals that have made an impact on my life. I am grateful for every person, place, or moment that has helped me to produce this book.

- First and foremost, thank you God for blessing me with a beautiful life and giving me this great responsibility to impact lives.

- To my wife, you are my rock. I can't begin to thank you enough for your love, support, and dedication. You are hilarious, and I love you!

- To my children, I am so proud of you all. You all bring me joy, and I am absolutely in love with you! I pray that my words will help you in your journeys.

- To all of my families, Wilsons, Wrights, Fields, Toomeys, Ackers, and Taverneses, thank you for all of the love and support.

- To my personal board of directors, thank you for your mentorship, guidance, friendship, and development.

- To my Charles Warner Projects and Boys & Girls Club of Jackson County families, I will not let you down. Thank you for shaping me.

- To all of my students and mentees, you are so special to me. Thank you for allowing me to invest in your lives.

- To everyone that submitted a survey, thank you for trusting me with your insecurities and life experiences. Your insights and words will help so many lives.

Turn on your light

FOREWORD
Turn on Your Light

This book is for every student in the world that has ever had a dream. Seneca has penned a book that will help millennials understand their worth, power, and purpose in this world. In his book, *Turn On Your Light*, Seneca challenges you to embrace the inner greatness within yourself. We all have greatness within us, the question is, will we use it? I've spoken in hundreds of schools across America, as well as internationally, and I can tell you that students from Middle Schools, High Schools, Colleges, and Universities are all the same. They have goals and want to accomplish great things, but many times question the possibilities. The agenda of this book is to remove any doubt that you may have about your worth and purpose in life.

Did you notice that the book isn't called, "How to Find Your Light", or "How to Get a Light"? The book isn't called "What to do When You Find A Light," is it? NO! The book is called "Turn on Your Light." The title itself is a mandate, an order, or command for you to access and use what is already placed inside of you. The light that's within you is symbolic of your purpose, passion, and power in this world. We all have a light within us, the question is, will you turn it on? Will you shine bright in a seemly dark, depressing, and dreary world? Think of what the world would look like when people like you decide to shine bright, and illuminate the world with their gifts, talent, light, and love!

I can understand the need for Seneca to write this book because many people today question their worth and value. They question the reason and purpose for their life. They question if they can truly accomplish great things, and question if their dreams can come true. For years I doubted my purpose, passion, and power. I, like Seneca, know how it feels to struggle in life, and come from poverty. I, like Seneca, know how it feels to have a void in your heart because your biological father isn't there. I, like Seneca, know how it feels to fail and feel like a failure. But guess what? I, like Seneca, bounced back and began to pursue the greatness within me. I turned on my light, and with a lot of hard work and dedication, made my dreams come true. It didn't happen right away, and it wasn't easy but eventually, in time, my light got brighter and brighter.

Most students that I speak with today have a hard time navigating through life because they feel that they can't see a way through. The challenges and hard times that life presents are like a constant cloud over their head. I get that. Here's my advice for you, don't be surprised by the darkness. Life at times can be and will be hard and challenging. There are times when you'll feel by yourself, but don't ever forget that you were born for this! You were born to make an impact in the world! You are the solution to a dark world, and the truth is that your purpose, passion, and power will shine bright in the world. You see, light illuminates most in darkness.

You should not be worried about the darkness, the darkness should be worried about you! You are a force to be reckoned with! You are more powerful than you know! The greatness within you is the very thing that this world needs. This is why Seneca has given you the command to *Turn On Your Light*, and to let that light shine bright. Your light will be used to illuminate the path for those who come behind you. Your light will be used to show others the beauty and power within them. There are people in class with you now that need you to shine bright so that they can see the possibilities within them. The time is perfect because the time is now. Turn on your light, and shine bright for the world to see!

- Jeremy J. Anderson

Turn on your Light

INTRODUCTION
Fulfilling Your Purpose

Have you ever had your light turned on? Having your light turned on is that aha moment, a paradigm shift, or a moment of truth, where someone or something that has inspired you to create action. I remember the first time my light was turned on like it was yesterday. It was in 2003, when I met Dr. Dennis Kimbro, a powerful motivational speaker and a professor at Clark Atlanta University in Atlanta, Georgia. Dr. Kimbro turned on my light when he said, "You have 18,632 days left on the earth. What are you going to do with the rest of them?"

It made me think about my life and my life's purpose. I knew I had a passion for people, mentoring, coaching, and spreading love to everyone I meet. Furthermore, I like to share my words and experiences to uplift others. After hearing Dr. Kimbro's speech, I had that aha moment. Dr. Kimbro turned on my light. I knew that day that I wanted to be a motivational speaker. I want to turn on other people's light.

Ever since that moment, I have been on a journey to fulfill my life's purpose. There have been many struggles, failures, and disappointments on my journey, but those trials and tribulations have made me stronger. My light shines brighter because of it. During my journey, I found out that you have to go through some things to have a more beautiful and brighter story to encourage and shine your light on others.

Are you looking to find and fulfill your purpose? Do you want to turn on your light and shine it brightly on the world? If so, this book is for you. This book is for anyone who is looking to move to the next level of their life. This book is for the person who is ready to start living their dreams. This book is for the individual who will shine their light on the world.

We are all blessed with a light inside of us, and this book will serve as a guide to help you search and dig deep within yourself to find that light. This book will help you find the necessary skills and tools you will need to fulfill your purpose. This book is a gift for you.

So, what are you waiting for? Dive into this book because your purpose is waiting for you!

TURN ON
YOUR LIGHT

*"You have to find what sparks a light in
you so that you in your own way
can illuminate the world."*
- Oprah Winfrey

*"Light must come from inside. You cannot
ask the darkness to leave; you must
turn on the light."*
– Sogyal Rinpoche

*"We are indeed the light of the world
— but only if our switch is turned on."*
– John Hagee

Chapter 1

DISCOVERING A DIFFERENT PATH

I used to feel that life dealt me an unfair hand. I was born into poverty with a single mom who was struggling to work a dead-end job and doing her best to raise her kids. The absence of a father had a huge impact on my life because I always felt lost, incomplete, and confused. It was extremely difficult experiencing moments for the first time without a father helping to guide me through life. Learning how to ride a bike, playing sports, shaving, or just talking to a girl I like were challenging for me. In addition, living in the projects for the majority of my life exposed me to an environment where I was surrounded by drugs, gangs and crime. Although I felt I had good community there, it did not provide me with many positive opportunities.

Furthermore, for most of my life I lacked confidence and felt uneducated and unsure of myself, so I didn't value education. But later I learned that I just didn't have the resources, tools, or guidance to put me in a position to succeed. My mom did the best she could, it was very difficult for her, never having finished high school, and always working to support the family. In addition, for the early part of my life, so many people in my environment spoke with broken English that I could never even know whether I was speaking correctly to others outside my community.

Overall, I felt like I was never good enough in almost every area in my life. I felt like I wasn't good enough to have a wife and a family. I felt like I wasn't good enough to own a home with a backyard. I felt like I wasn't good enough to attend college and graduate. I felt like I wasn't good enough for a successful career. I felt like I wasn't good enough to be wealthy. I felt like I was never good enough to be the true me.

However, I am here today to tell you that I am good enough. I am good enough and so much more. There have been people, places and moments in my life that helped me recognize my light, and that I am powerful beyond measure. Life is about taking the hand you were dealt and making the best out of it. You may not be able to control the cards you were dealt, but you are most certainly responsible for the results.

We have a choice in life to be a light in the world, and I choose to be blessed. Now I am fortunate to serve as a motivational speaker, author, poet, coach, adjunct professor and college educator. I have a bachelor's degree, a master's degree, and a very successful career in Student Affairs. I am outspoken and very confident. Throughout my life, I have developed vehicles to fulfill my purpose. It is now my responsibility to serve, to "pay it forward" and use those same vehicles to motivate as many young people as I can to be college and career ready.

Chapter 2

THE LIGHT SWITCH

You have 18,632 days left on this earth. What are you going to do with the rest of them?

That question turned on a light in my head for the first time in my life. It was January 27, 2003 when Dr. Dennis Kimbro gave a motivational speech at a conference to a group of 150 emerging students. You could hear the silence in the room as he asked that question. For me, it was like I had finally paid the light bill and Dr. Kimbro worked for the electric company. He was the electrician who came to make the connection in my mind. Can you imagine me counting on my fingers? I thought to myself, 18,632 days is not a lot of days to have left.

When I was younger, my only goal in life was to be the first person in my family and my neighborhood to graduate from a four-year university. My mother was a single mom with four kids. We never had much, but we had love. We lived in Charles Warner Projects in Pascagoula, Mississippi. Though the projects are supposed to be temporary housing, we somehow managed to make it home for more than 20 years.

Living in the projects taught me how to over-come barriers in my life, how to deal with ad-versity, how to survive. But I learned how to love from my mom. Like I said, we didn't have much, especially during Christmas and other holidays, but my mother always found ways to give gifts to other kids who had even less. She baked cakes for other kids' birthdays in the neighborhood. My Mom's motto is, "Baby if you got it, give it; but if you can't, there is nothing you can do." I didn't understand it then, but I do now. I love my mother and I always wanted to make her proud, so I went to the University of Southern Mississippi, (USM).

I made it to college, but I didn't have the slight-est clue of what I was doing until I met my boss, Chris McGee. Chris was the assistant director of facilities for the campus recreation center at USM, and he gave me my first job as a college student as a facility supervisor of the Payne Center. At work one day; Chris looked at me and said, "Boy! What are you going to do with the rest of your life?" I did not have an answer, so Chris took me under his wing, molded me into a professional, and introduced me to the field of campus rec-reation. Chris would take me to conferences for my student development. It was at my first con-ference that I met Dr. Dennis Kimbro, the mental electrician. Ever since that day in January, I knew I wanted to be a mental electrician, too.

Following the formative example set by my mom, I want to give back. Like Dr. Dennis Kimbro, I want to turn on other people's light. Like my boss, Chris McGee, I want to create that aha moment, a paradigm shift, a moment truth, where I inspire people to create action. And that is what I want to do for you. I want to be your mental electrician.

FOUNDATION OF YOUR SOURCE

"You can't build a great building on a weak foundation. You must have a solid foundation if you're going to have a strong superstructure."
- Gordon B. Hinckley

"Life isn't just about darkness or light, rather it's about finding light within the darkness."
- Landon Parham

When you find your purpose, it will need to be built on top of your foundation. Your foundation is the source of your strength. Do you know where your strength comes from?

In order to be successful, you must have a strong foundation. You can't build your purpose on a shaky foundation. At the core of your truth, your foundation is who you are.

Who or what has helped shape that foundation in your life? Is it God, a parent, a family member or friend, a mentor, a place, or a moment in time in your life? Whatever it is, you must identify it to help find your purpose and to shine your light brightly. Your foundation is the place you will visit when the journey to your purpose becomes challenging and confusing. It is the place you dwell in when you want to quit. It is also the place you go when you are celebrating your accomplishments and your best moments. This place is your home.

Chapter 3

GOD FIRST

My relationship with God hasn't always been the strongest, especially when I was in my early twenties. There were many times back then when I felt like I should have been in jail or even dead. I recall driving my friends around with their often carrying drugs and guns and all of us probably drinking. I wasn't a bad person, but my friends and I were making some very poor choices. But through all of my foolishness, He has always been there for me.

To be candid, I felt like He always was there and I was either too scared or didn't want to acknowledge it. But all my life it has seemed like I have a spiritual guardian watching over me.

God has waited on me. He had a plan and purpose for my life. I have accepted that plan and I have allowed Him to serve as the foundation of my life.

God is the source of my strength, and I put Him first in everything I do. It is important to understand that you were given a gift at birth, and through that gift you will be able to fulfill your purpose. In the Bible, John 8:12 God said, "I am the light of the world. Whoever follows me will never walk in darkness but will have the light of life." God has lit my lamp and has allowed me to shine it on the world.

When I experience doubts in my life, I put my faith over fear. I look to the Word, because He said that He didn't give me the spirit of fear, that the Word is the Lamp unto my feet and the light unto my path. Throughout my journey, God has given me the strength to fulfill my purpose, and through Him I know all things are possible. I have built my life on faith, and God serves as the first layer of my foundation

Chapter 4

A MOTHER'S LOVE

When people ask why I am so kind and caring toward people. I tell them that I learned it from my mother, that it was "embedded into my soul". When I was growing up I watched how hard my mother worked to make sure she took care of her kids. In 1982 she was a single mom with 3 children, living with her sister, my aunt Creole in Moss Point, Mississippi while working at Wendy's in nearby Pascagoula. My mother didn't have transportation, so most of the time she walked to work. To this day I can't believe she would walk 5 miles to work, even for a 3-hour shift. The trip was an hour and a half each way. She had to walk in the rain, even during thunderstorms.

Often, I wonder what my mom thought about on her walks to work. Did she think about why she was doing this? Was she scared, especially at night? Was this job worth it or did she want to give up and quit?

When I was a child, my mom didn't talk much about her experiences walking to work. But as

I got older, she did mention some frustrations and incidents. One story I remember was of an encounter she had with a dog. On her walk down Shortcut Road in the City of Moss Point one morning, she stood face to face with a big black dog. My mom is terrified of dogs, but she said there was something different about this dog. She said that the dog looked at her and she looked at it, and she was so surprised when the dog started walking beside her. She felt like the dog was guiding her to work, like it was protecting her from something. This dog walked all the way with her until a friend stopped and picked her up, less than a few blocks away from her job. She said the experience was very strange, but that she felt safe. And she was safe. I feel very grateful for that dog on that day.

Every now and then my mom would receive rides to work, but when she finally got her first car, she would pick up everybody that needed a ride. One day I asked my mom why she picked up everyone she saw, and she replied, "Baby, I know how it feels to need a ride". She added, "I also know how it feels to ask someone for a ride and have to sit around and wait on them". She would drive everyone everywhere and would not take any gas money when they offered it to her. It was funny to watch some people try to throw money in the car as she drove away, and her throwing it back out the window as she drove off. My mom believes that you shouldn't take money from anyone that needs a ride, especially if you are driving in the same direction. She would tell me how, before she had her car, it was hard for her to pay people for rides, and how she felt guilty for not being able to offer any gas money. My mother never wanted anyone else to feel that way, like she was taking advantage of them.

After my mom moved out of my Aunt's house a few years later, I remember moving from apartment to apartment, until we moved into the Charles Warner Projects. I know the Projects are supposed to be temporary, but we made it into a home. When we first moved to the Projects, Charles Warner was known as the "white folks project" because it was mostly white people who lived there.

We were one of the first Black families to move into Charles Warner Projects and it wasn't the best experience for us. One day, she was told by a white neighbor that people were talking about hurting her and her kids, even that they were going to burn a cross in our yard. My mom was scared, especially when she had to leave us home by ourselves while she went to work. But she told us that she wasn't going to let anyone run us off and no harm came to us while living in Charles Warner Projects.

Over time, the projects shifted to a Black community. Even though we were well respected, we still had to worry about crime that was happening all around us. Though we had great people in our community, we were not immune from fights, shootouts, and drug activity.

After many years of working at Wendy's, my mother found a better paying job at the glove factory, at least until the plant closed seven years later. At the time, I didn't understand because I was young, but living in the Projects were people even poorer than us. Being a kid, it was difficult to appreciate it when my mom turned into Mother Teresa, trying to help everyone in the Projects. All we saw was her giving other kids all of these gifts for Christmas and other holidays while we got only a few of things we wanted. My sister and I used to be so jealous! As I became older, I realized that those gifts we saw my mom giving were only dollar gifts, but at the time it seemed like so much more. My mom would explain later that there was something very fulfilling about giving. She would say, "We are supposed to bless others."

One year, my mom took a night class for cake decorating, and she found a passion for baking cakes and cookies. She did it for fun but became very good at baking and decorating cakes. Somehow our neighbors found out how good the cakes were and started asking her to bake one for them. She began baking cakes for almost everyone in the Projects for their birthdays. Random people would come to our house and tell my mom that their son's or daughter's birthday was that week and asked if she would bake a cake for them. "Who is paying for these cakes?" I would think. I felt that people were taking advantage of her, but it was just something she loved to do.

I can go on and on about my mom, but one of my most favorite things I can remember is how she loved everybody in the Projects the same way as if they were her own children, even the kids who got into a lot of trouble. My mom is a faithful Christian woman. She walks by faith. She used to stop the kids that some would call gangstas, in the middle of the streets and ask them to pray with her. And they would do it every time, because they respected her like that.

After all these years, my mom is still giving more love to everyone she meets. She would always tell me, "Baby, if you got it, give it, and it would be given back to you!" I am blessed to have a mother who loves like God does. She was given an eternal light and she continues to shine it on the world. How can I not strive to be like her and Give More Love? My mother has shaped my life and has helped me add another layer to my strong foundation.

Turn on your light

Chapter 5

THE TRANSFORMATION

The Boys and Girls Club of Jackson County, Mississippi saved my life.

In the projects, if we weren't getting into trouble or playing basketball, there wasn't much else to do. However, in 1992, the boys and girls club moved into the Charles Warner Projects. I believe I was the club's first member. I remember the day the club opened its doors like it was yesterday. I stood outside that door for at least two hours waiting on them to open.

The club had a pool table, table tennis, foosball, bumper pool and a portable basketball hoop. We also received juice and cookies almost every day, too. I was in heaven. Another great part about the club was its being directly behind our house. I went there almost every day.

The club became very popular in Charles Warner Projects. The staff started building programming for the members. It gave us kids structure. The staff built an after-school program to help us with our homework. We created the Torch Club, which helped to meet the special character and development needs of boys and girls ages 11 to 13, and Keystone Club, which provided leadership development opportunities for young people ages 14 to 18. They were built to empower students to have a voice. We developed organized sports to compete against other clubs and learn how to be a team. We went on field trips to explore. We were exposed to opportunities we would never have experienced outside the club.

I remember our first field trip out of state, to Styx Rivers in Alabama. I had never been out of the state without my family and it was a new water park for me as well. I had the time of my life. We had so much fun at the water park, but my most favorite trip was camping in Hazelhurst, Mississippi. The members of the Keynote clubs were provided the opportunity to spend a weekend at the camp. I had never stayed away from mom for a weekend, at least without family. It was an experience to remember. We fished. We ate. We played games. We canoed. We lit fires. We hiked. We told stories. We ate which I believe I already mentioned, but the food was so good I had to mention it twice. We had so much fun. Those were the days.

The Boys and Girls Club was fun, but it was fun because of the Staff. I remember every person that worked at the club. They were all caring people and they let us know that they loved us. My favorite has always been Ms. Catherine Glaude. She was a counselor at the Charles Warner unit when I started and currently serves as the Chief Professional Officer of the Boys and Girls Club of Jackson county. She is like my second mom. I used to be at the club so much, my mom started asking "who is this Catherine Glaude? I need to meet her." Ms. Cat, as we used to call her, helped me to start believing in myself. She helped me to start having confidence and to speak up for myself. She helped develop me into a better person. When I turned 16, she also gave me the opportunity to work at the club during the summers until I was able to be an official staff member.

Working at the Boys and Girls Club taught me the importance of serving and giving back. I loved every minute of working there. I guess I saw those kids as me. It was a blessing to put so many smiles on the kids face. Everything I was taught, I was able to share with my kids. I was happy I had an opportunity to possibly add value or uplift my boys and girls club kids.

I truly believe the Boys and Girls Club saved my life and developed me as a person. It showed me that we are here to serve others and to help to develop our kids. The club taught me that if we don't do it, no one will. The Boys and Girls Club built onto my foundation and made me a stronger person.

Chapter 6

THE MENTORSHIP

*Boy! What are you going to do with
the rest of your life?*

Those words ring in the back of my mind constantly. Imagine a 6'6" 320-pound intimidating Black man staring down in my face, waiting for an answer. Young and confused, I never thought about life after college. My only goal was to graduate from a four-year university, but in 2002 I met Chris McGee.

Chris was at the time Assistant Director of Facilities for Recreational Sports at the University of Southern Mississippi. He was my supervisor, my mentor, and my dad. Growing up in a single-parent home he was the closest person to a father figure that I had ever known.

Chris is one of those guys that knows everyone. When he meets someone new, he asks their name and where they are from. Then he'll say something like, "Boy, I know your uncle, you are Bobby Johnson's son or you are Betty Jean's daughter I went to school with your Momma". Chris was funny, and it is easy to talk with him. However, Chris is also one of those old-school, hard-nosed, do-what-I-tell-you-because-I-said-so type of bosses. He believes you work with your hands and that personal experiences are the best teacher. Chris never gave answers. He showed us problems and situations, and would ask in his strong deep voice, "Now! Tell me what's wrong with this picture?" and then just stand there until we figured it out.

Chris was tough, but he loved us. It was at the most vital time in my life when he asked me, "What are you going to do for the rest of your life?" and I had no answer. Chris introduced me to the field of campus recreation and NIRSA: Leaders in Collegiate Recreation. He showed me that there was a career in campus recreation if I wanted it. He started taking me to local and regional student development conferences. Then, in 2005 he invited me to attend the national conference in Orlando, Florida, where I could possibly attain a graduate assistant position. I didn't know anything about writing a resume, interviewing, or looking professional. Chris taught me how to write a resume, developed my interviewing skills, and cleaned up my image. He believed in being presentable and sociable. Chris would always tell us, "It's not what you know, it's who you know and who knows you."

I was nervous about attending the national conference. I had never even owned a suit or tie, but Chris said, "Son, don't worry about that I will take care of that." He took me to his house, opened his closet and handed me my very first jacket, an oversized, out of style brown blazer with suede patches on the elbows. I didn't want to seem ungrateful, but I told Chris that I didn't feel comfortable wearing the blazer. Chris is the type of person where it is very difficult to hurt his feelings so he just responded, "Well bring your ass on, let's go to the store."

Chris took me to a local store, picked out and handed me a blue blazer from the rack. I looked at the $90 price tag then at Chris and said, "I don't have $90". Chris turned to me with a stern face and said "I know that, I am buying the damn blazer". I was totally overwhelmed that someone would spend that much money for me. I was probably more shocked that someone cared that much for me and that someone believed that much in me. Leaving the store, I told Chris that I would pay him back, but he told me to "pay him back by paying it forward." He said, "When you have the space and ability to do the same thing for another student that may be in similar shoes, that is how you will pay me back". I have been paying Chris back ever since.

I truly believe everyone has a purpose and ev-erything happens for a reason. I was blessed to have crossed paths with Chris McGee because he was the light I needed at that time. He gave me that spark and showed me how important it is to be the light and shine my light on others. Chris and his mentorship provided another layer to my foundation by being a caring mentor and dad to a confused young man that needed it most at the time.

Chapter 7

THE MENTAL ELECTRICIAN

D r. Kimbro also showed up at just the right time in my life. I was lost. I was not living, I was only existing. Like I mentioned earlier, my only goal in life was to graduate from a four university. I never thought about any plans after I would graduate. Basically, through my lens, life would be over after I graduated. My small thinking was challenged by Dr. Dennis Kimbro's speech. That pivotal day in 2003, Dr. Kimbro spoke to my soul. He spoke with conviction, easily captivating the audience with his powerful vocal tone and range. Everyone was on the edge of their seats, grabbing a hold of every word Dr. Kimbro delivered. At the time, I had never heard anyone speak with so much passion and power.

After the conference, I researched everything I could find about Dr. Dennis Kimbro. I bought and read all of his books. My favorite book of Dr. Kimbro's is *What Makes the Great, Great!* I have probably read that book about 10 times. In the book, Dr. Kimbro talks about how he started a journey by interviewing several Black successful people. He wanted to know the strategies used to make the great, great. There are so many great stories in the book, but I really enjoyed one about a legendary washwoman. Dr. Kimbro starts his last chapter, titled *The Greatest Story Ever Told: Leaving a Legacy*, with the story of the phenomenal Black woman, Oseola McCarty. Ms. McCarty was a local lifelong washwoman in Hattiesburg, Mississippi who quit school in the sixth grade and would go on to donate $150,000 to the University of Southern Mississippi. Her donation provided scholarships for black students in need of financial assistance. It is a powerful story. At the time I was actually living on campus in the new Oseola McCarty dorm, but did not have a clue of her legacy. I also didn't know Ms. McCarty was the second cousin of my close friend Jackie McCarty. I strongly encourage you to read *What Makes the Great, Great,* and explore the legacy of Oseola McCarty.

One of my favorite moments with Dr. Dennis Kimbro came a few years later at another conference, where he was the presenter and I was the session monitor and had the great honor to introduce him. It was one of the best highlights for me. I was nervous, but I was more excited than anything. After his amazing presentation, we took a picture together and I was able to pick his brain for a few minutes. He was very engaged in our conservation and further encouraged me to find and live my purpose.

This exchange with my idol gave me such a boost in motivation to be like him, to impact people and to turn on their light. I continue to follow Dr. Kimbro and look forward to inspiring millions of young people to turn on their light and to live their purpose. That moment with Dr. Dennis Kimbro changed my life and helped me lay down another layer onto my foundation.

Exercise: Take a moment to identify the foundation of your life and explain why this person, place, thing and/or moment has helped shape you and your foundation.

_____

_____

_____

_____

_____

_____

_____

_____

_____

_____

_____

_____

_____

_____

_____

BE THE LIGHT

"Be the light that helps others see."
- Anonymous

"You may think your light is small, but it can make a huge difference in other people's lives."
– Anonymous

"The meaning of life is to find your gift. The purpose of life is to give it away."
- Pablo Picasso

Chapter 8

YOU ARE GOOD ENOUGH

If I were to say to you, "Are you good enough?", what would you say?

At some point in our lives we will experience failures, setbacks, and disappointments. However, these experiences make us stronger. We are who we are because of them. We all have similar problems, though we face different situations and receive different outcomes. You may not be able to control the cards you are dealt but you most certainly can control the results. We have the ability to choose how we feel and respond to the challenges in our life. Someone once said, "10% of life is what happens to you, 90% is how you respond to it". We should choose to be blessed.

There have been many times in my life where I felt as if I wasn't good enough for my purpose, that I was a failure or that I didn't belong. Many people played a part in making me feel that way. Whether it was a teacher, a coach, friends, a family member, or an ex-partner, they all have contributed to my insecurities. I wanted to know if I was the only person who felt this way, so I decided to do research. I conducted a survey to identify moments in other people's lives when they have felt as if they weren't good enough and how they responded to those feelings. With this information I could explore solutions to help others as they are going through moments of doubt and insecurity. I interviewed over 50 people, and asked them the following questions:

1. Have you ever felt like you were not good enough?
   a. If so, what was the situation?

2. In that situation, how did you respond to your feelings?

3. What were the results?

4. What would be your best advice to someone who is feeling as if they were not good enough?

5. What do you think are some of the reasons people may feel as if they are not good enough?

6. Has someone ever told you that you weren't good enough?

7.   Did you believe them? Why or why not?

8.   What would a person need to feel as if they were good enough?

9.   What area(s) in your life do you feel (or have felt) as if you are not good enough?

10.   If you were to describe how it felt to not be good enough what words would you use?

11.   When you felt this way, who or what motivated you to feel otherwise?

After receiving the data from the survey, I was amazed to find out that there is no new feeling under the sun. I was not alone. I concluded that 98% of the people who responded felt like they weren't good enough at some point in their life.

Here are some areas where people felt like they were not good enough.
Their relationships, parents, education, health, job or career, finances, physical appearance, social life, spirituality, and/or through sports.

Here are some reasons why people felt that they are not good enough.
Fear, comparison, being told, rejection, low self-esteem, experiencing a failure or loss, self-depreciation, depression, codependency, social anxiety, and/or mental or physical abuse.

Here are some feelings of when we feel that we were not good enough.
Heaviness, burdensomeness, sadness, depression, frustration, devalued, invisible, unappreciated, failure, uneducated, degraded, defeated, incompetent, lack of courage, and/or powerless.

Here are some areas to make you feel good enough.
Love, acceptance, joy, hope, believing in something, action plan, focus on self, looking at your strengths, listen to a motivational talk, talking to someone for positive encouragement, realizing and accepting your feelings, meditation, reading self-help books, close friends and family, small groups and/or God and prayer.

When someone tells you that you are not good enough, use that as motivation to prove them wrong. If you believe you are not enough, the same rule applies. If you are your own hardest critic, what makes you any different from those naysayers? You may doubt and question yourself daily but you must learn to use those doubts as motivation to prove *yourself* wrong. Every morning I remind myself that I am good enough to do what I love.

Your failures, pain, struggles, fears, setbacks, and barriers are only temporary, a short segment of time in your life. Don't stop at your pain, failures, fears, struggles, setbacks, or barriers. Push through them and get to the winner's circle. There are many people hanging around with failure like it's their best friend. Failure, fear, pain, struggles, setbacks, and barriers are not your friends, they are your teachers. Learn the lesson and move on towards greatness and your purpose. Remember you are good enough to do what you love!

I challenge you to take the survey. It will be beneficial for you and it will provide some healing.

---

1. Please go to www.senecawilson.com and share your survey results with me. In the appendix to this book there are a few stories from some of the people who took the first survey. You may find them interesting.

Turn on your Light

Chapter 9

COMFORTABLE WITH BEING UNCOMFORTABLE

D o you like being uncomfortable? You know, that awkward feeling of nervousness, discomfort, and anxiety that makes you feel like you are in one of those old Southwest Airlines commercials, "Wanna get away?" Well, for the majority of my life I didn't like being in uncomfortable situations, especially speaking in front of people. Believe it or not I was terrified of speaking in front of people.

My worst experience was as an undergrad, when I had to deliver a presentation to my Sports Law class. I knew the material, but all that came out of my mouth were 'ums', 'you knows' and 'know what I am saying', which I pronounced as "nahmsayin". It was bad enough that my teacher said things like, "No we don't know, so why don't you tell us?" and "No, we don't know what you are trying to say". About two minutes into the presentation, my professor told me to sit down and that I could try it again next week. I felt so embarrassed, I wanted to disappear.

Fear can be a great motivator when it makes you feel like you are not good enough. Fear of failure and success makes us feel uncomfortable. When we are feeling uncomfortable, we either allow ourselves to grow or continue to hold ourselves captive to mediocrity. In order to remove our personal insecurities, we need to practice being comfortable with being uncomfortable.

During my time working at Syracuse University, I took a course with a nontraditional professor who intentionally made all his students uncomfortable in class. If you were late, you had to do a random presentation in front of the class. Out of nowhere, he would ask a student, "Tell me what is wrong with the room," or "Tell me what happened in a different country today". He would ask us nonsense questions like, "what's your 168". It made us feel uncomfortable, embarrassed and/or incompetent. The professor told us that the reason he did this is because he wanted us to be comfortable with being uncomfortable.

Believe it or not it worked, because by the end of the semester we were always prepared to speak or answer a question without being nervous, embarrassed, or uncomfortable. In addition, he taught us discipline because no one was ever late after the first two weeks. He taught us to read the newspaper and be aware of current events and foreign affairs. He taught us to be aware of our surroundings and how to better "manage our 168".

Sometimes we have to intentionally put ourselves into uncomfortable situations, so that we are faced with challenges that help us move away from mediocrity and toward success and our purpose. Being comfortable with being uncomfortable is about enabling your light to shine bright. It reminds me of the quote from Marianne Williams -

"Our deepest fear is not that we are inadequate. Our deepest fear is that we are powerful beyond measure. It is our light, not our darkness that most frightens us. We ask ourselves, 'Who am I to be brilliant, gorgeous, talented, fabulous?' Actually, who are you not to be? You are a child of God. Your playing small does not serve the world. There is nothing enlightened about shrinking so that other people won't feel insecure around you. We are all meant to shine, as children do. We were born to make manifest the glory of God that is within us. It's not just in some of us; it's in everyone. And as we let our own light shine, we unconsciously give other people permission to do the same. As we are liberated from our own fear, our presence automatically liberates others."

I have always felt like I had a gift for speaking, but my fear and anxiety always got in the way of my light. It wasn't until I challenged myself by joining a toastmaster's class at Syracuse University that my gift for speaking came to light. I was able to put myself in uncomfortable situations to become more comfortable speaking in front of people. I am still always nervous speaking, but now I am more comfortable with it.

What's your fear? What makes you uncomfortable? I challenge you to conquer your fears by positioning yourself in uncomfortable situations. Practice being comfortable with being uncomfortable.

Exercise: What are 3 of your fears?

- _____
  _____
  _____
  _____
  _____
  _____

- _____
  _____
  _____
  _____
  _____
  _____

●

_____

_____

_____

_____

_____

_____

Exercise: Now explain how you are going to position yourself to be comfortable with being uncomfortable.

●

_____

_____

_____

_____

_____

●

_____

_____

_____

_____

_____

●

_____

_____

_____

_____

_____

Turn on your light—

Chapter 10

RICH IN PEOPLE

It pays to treat people with respect and love. It takes minimum effort to be nice to others or serve others and it really goes a long way. Service and kindness are like boomerangs, if you do it the right way, they always come back to you.

Most people associate being rich with having money, but I am rich in people. People are a little like investments. We invest our time, money, knowledge, and love in a person. However, you have to invest without looking for something in return, understanding that most likely it will be returned in another form or fashion.

When I first moved to Syracuse, the kids would come out to play basketball almost every day in my neighborhood, and I would go out to play with them every now and then. I am not as good of a basketball player as I used to be, but I would still have a great time with the kids.

There was a kid named Mark. Mark wasn't actually from the neighborhood, but he would always be out at the courts. He would come over to his aunt's house after school until his mother came to get him after work. Mark was 13 years old. One day he asked me if I would be willing to help develop his basketball skills so he could make the middle school basketball team. Of course I said yes. I spoke with his mom, who agreed. That day, I officially became Mark's mentor.

About a month later, when I was riding on the public bus headed to work, an older woman missed the last step in getting off of the bus and fell to the ground. She hurt herself badly. I quickly jumped off the bus along with the bus driver to assist and to see if she was okay. Nobody else on the bus was concerned about this woman. As a matter of fact, they were mad because they were going to miss the line-up downtown to catch their next bus. We stayed there for a while waiting for the ambulance, as many people grew impatient and started getting off the bus stepping right over the woman. It was very disappointing to witness.

A couple of weeks later, I rushed out of my house trying to get to the bus stop and as soon as the bus pulled up, I realized I left my wallet and didn't have any money to ride the bus. I asked if anyone could spare $1.25 for the ride, and it was like there were crickets on that bus. But suddenly out of nowhere the same woman who fell earlier stood up and said, "I will give you the $1.25". I told her thank you, but she quickly replied "No, thank you because you were the only person who helped me up when I fell". So, during our ride, we talked about many things, like her nephew, who always came over to play ball. I mentioned that I went out to play with the kids and that I have been mentoring another kid named Mark. She quickly said "MARK! He is my nephew, so you are Seneca. He talks about you all of the time". She said, "thank you for mentoring him, he needs a good role model in his life, and I have heard nothing but great things about you." As she was getting off the bus, she invited me over for dinner, and it was the start of a good relationship.

Mahatma Gandhi said that "the best way to find yourself, is to lose yourself in the service of others." It pays to treat people with respect, love and kindness because it really goes a long way. Be sure to invest in people and watch the return on your investment.

Power of Service
If you want to be great, learn the power of service. Ask yourself, how are you making someone's life better? Service should be a responsibility. Whether it is being a mentor for our youth, advocating for a cause, or serving food to the homeless, anyone can serve.

Dr. Martin Luther King Jr. said, "Everyone has the power for greatness — not for fame, but greatness, because greatness is determined by service." You owe it to yourself to serve, and in the words of Dr. Dennis Kimbro, "Service is the price you pay for the space you occupy. So, be great and serve!

Chapter 11

I SEE YOU

Many people ask me, why do you say hi to everybody you see? I could give several answers, such as that's how I was raised, I am from the south or I am a happy person. Those are all true, but the most important reason is because I want to let people know that I notice them. I want to let them know that they are not invisible. I want to let them know someone cares about them.

In 2006 at Oakland University someone wrote me a letter thanking me for stopping and saying hello, and giving them a hug. It said, "I was at one of the lowest points of my life and I felt like no one noticed me or cared about me. God must have used you because that was exactly what I needed at that time." We never know what people are going through, or how they are feeling in their lives. There are probably so many souls walking around waiting to be noticed.

We are living in a society where many people are walking around plugged into their earphones, locked into text and social media just to feel connected. We are so adapted to avoiding human interactions that we could save a life by sharing a simple smile, by saying hello, by giving a hug, by giving a high five, by sharing some encouraging words, or by just giving more love. There are so many people waiting or wishing someone would say to them that I see you. I. SEE. YOU. You may just save someone's life.

Give More Love

Love is exactly what the world needs. It is like water to plants; it helps us grow. Love is the reason the earth spins on its axis. It is not just a four-letter word; it is who we are. It is the time you spend with your loved ones, the simple smiles and hellos in the mornings, and the gifts you give to others because you are fortunate to do so. Try it! I challenge you to love more, to love your friends, to love your enemy, to love people, and to love yourself more. Gandhi said, "Be the change that you want to see in the world." Today give someone a hug, a high-five, a handshake, a smile, encouraging words, a gift or money if you are able to do so. Be the light in someone's world, you might just save a life.

DEVELOP YOUR LIGHT

"Growth is the great separator between those who succeed and those who do not. When I see a person beginning to separate themselves from the pack, it's almost always due to personal growth."
- John C. Maxwell

"Investing in yourself is the best investment you will ever make. It will not only improve your life, it will improve the lives of all those around you."
- Robin Sharma

"Luck is what happens when preparation meets opportunity."
- Lucius Annaeus Seneca

Chapter 12

UNDERSTANDING YOUR WHY

D o you know what you want to do for the rest of your life? Do you want to be a Mechanic, a Barber, or maybe a Motivational Speaker? What are you passionate about? What do you love? It is important to know what you want to be in life, to know what your purpose is, to know what you want to do for the rest of your life. However, I believe it is more important to understand why it is your purpose, and to understand why you want to be or do what you love for the rest of your life.

As a motivational speaker, I am not just sharing words. I understand that I am helping you turn on your light. I am helping you find your passion and purpose in life. I am helping you build a better lifestyle. I am helping you know what you want to be in life, and to help you understand why it is your purpose.

A mechanic, for example, is not just fixing cars. When a mechanic understands why it is their purpose, a mechanic understands that they are helping families. They are helping you get to work the next day in order for you to keep your job, so you can put food on the table. When they have their *Why* they know they are helping you pick up your kids from daycare every day. Mechanics are ensuring your car and your family are safe every time you are on the road.

A barber or stylist doesn't just cut hair. When a barber or stylist understands their purpose, they understand that they are building up your self-esteem. They are giving you the confidence to get that next job. They understand that you have a personal brand and it matters how you look. They are preparing you to meet your future partner. So, when you find out what you want to do for the rest of your life, make sure you understand why.

Chapter 13

2020 VISION

What is your vision? Do you have a vision? Vision is defined as the act or power of anticipating that which will or may come to be. It is important to know what you want out of life. It is important to know that you can accomplish a goal you want to achieve. So, what do you want to do with your life? Who do you want to become? If you don't have a vision you may want to find one. If you have one keep working toward that vision. Put yourself around the right people and places that will help you carry out your vision. Remember, everyone will not understand where you are going, but have faith, keep believing and keep moving forward. Don't allow people to change who you have already set out to be. It is your vision! Go for it!

Believe in your vision. You and God are the only ones that will fully understand it. People may even interfere with your being successful because they do not understand your vision. They will try to change your vision to fit their understanding. If God wants other people to understand your vision, He will reveal it to them. If you have a vision keep the faith and believe in your vision.

It is amazing how clear your vision gets when you turn on the lights. When you can clearly see where you are going, you are able to get to your destination faster and more safely. When you create your vision, you are turning on the light to your purpose. My good friend Tariq turned on his light.

Tariq was a student at Syracuse University working at a barber shop on campus. Tariq was my barber, and in 2013 he told me he was going to be a celebrity barber. At the time neither I nor the other barbers in the shop understood what that really meant, but Tariq had turned on the light to his purpose.

Tariq was a very good barber when I met him, but once he understood and stated his vision, many things changed for him. Tariq began to work more on his craft. He attended barbers' clinics, shows, and conferences. Tariq started branding everything he did with his brand, Groomsmith. He would take pictures and videos of his haircuts and share them on social media. He was also cutting the Syracuse Men's basketball team's hair, claiming that he was the official barber of the SU men's basketball team. This would earn him a lot of notoriety around the university.

At the time, it seemed like all of the students at

the university were coming to Tariq. Other barbers in the shop started to take notice of the success Tariq was having with his vision. Then, when an SU player, one of Tariq's clients, made it to the NBA. And just like that, Tariq officially became a celebrity's barber.

Once Tariq reached his goal, he didn't stop there. Tariq started maximizing his vision by preparing to offer services that no one was offering in men's barber shops, like steam facials, lining eyebrows and shampooing heads. He was determined to fulfill his purpose. Tariq became a perfectionist for his purpose. Literally, my haircuts went from 30 minutes to an hour and a half sometimes because Tariq was trying to perfect his craft.

On one of the biggest days of my life Tariq made sure I looked better than I had ever looked before. It was the morning of my wedding and Tariq was masterful with his clippers. He examined my hair like he was preparing for a surgery. For Tariq, I am sure it was because he knew his Why. He knew this wasn't just a haircut. He knew that this was a very special moment in my life, and he wanted to ensure my hair made a statement. Tariq started my day off with great confidence. He made me feel good about myself. More important, he made me look damn good. I was ready to take on the journey with my beautiful wife. I received so many compliments on my hair that day, and every time I look back at my wedding pictures, I can't help but notice the haircut.

Tariq received his big break when he was hired on to be one of the official barbers for the movie Barbershop 2. Tariq has cut many famous NBA players, NFL players, actors and entertainers' hair. Tariq did it! He turned on his light, and now he is helping other barbers turn on their light as well.

Chapter 14

BELIEVE IN SOMETHING

To get to your life's destination, you have to believe in something. If you don't believe in anything, how can you really live your best life? Your beliefs shape your character and mold your personality. They help serve as a road map toward your truth.

It is important to identify your beliefs so that you can align them with your thoughts, attitude, and behavior. When they all become one, it will move you toward a happier life.

Below is a list of my personal beliefs. I use them to help guide my life. I also share my beliefs with my children in hopes that they will develop similar personal beliefs as they get older. I encourage you to develop your own list to help you get to your destiny.

Believe in God:
because God is the creator of all things, and through God all things are possible.

Believe in yourself:
because you are a child of God. Always have confidence in yourself that you can achieve anything.

Believe in your family:
because family will be there to support you. And family doesn't only mean blood. Family is whomever you call family.

Believe in hard work:
because if you want to be great you have to work hard for it. Never let anyone outwork you.

Believe in education:
because it is important to seek knowledge and educate yourself daily and understand that you don't need a degree to be educated.

Believe in networking:
because networking is one of the most powerful tools of achieving your goals. As often said, it isn't what you know, but who you know and who knows you. Also, who you know will get you in the door, but what you know will keep you there.

Believe in your health:
because if you are not healthy nothing else matters. Take care of yourself so you can be the best you.

Believe in financial literacy:
because it leads to financial freedom. Always pay yourself first, minimize your liabilities and capitalize on your assets. Learn how to provide and sustain wealth for you and your family.

Believe in responsibility:
because we all make mistakes. It happens. Own up to your mistakes or your mistakes will own you.

Believe in service:
because we were all put here to serve in some capacity. Help others get the things that they want, and your life will be much greater because of it.

What are your beliefs? Please list them in the section below.

- _____
  _____
  _____
  _____

- _____
  _____
  _____
  _____

- _____
  _____
  _____
  _____

- _____
  _____
  _____
  _____

- _____
  _____
  _____
  _____

- _____
  _____
  _____
  _____

- _____
  _____
  _____
  _____

- _____
  _____
  _____
  _____

- _____
  _____
  _____
  _____

- _____
  _____
  _____
  _____

- _____
  _____
  _____
  _____

- _____
  _____
  _____
  _____

- _____
  _____
  _____
  _____

- _____
  _____
  _____
  _____

Chapter 15

4 Ps TO SUCCEED

Do you ever wonder what separates successful people from unsuccessful people? It is what I call the 4 Ps to succeed. The 4 Ps are preparation, practice, persistence and performance. These 4 Ps are a clear pathway to success. There are several people looking for "microwave success," a short cut to performance. You can't cheat success. You have to put in the work. Talent alone doesn't support a strong foundation. Talent alone doesn't necessarily have all of the essential fundamentals required to succeed. When you are looking for long term success it starts with the 4 Ps.

Preparation

If you want to build anything, a strong foundation is essential. Preparation allows you to build a solid foundation and stand firmly on your performance. It allows you to be consistent with your performance. The great Zig Ziglar said, "Success occurs when opportunity meets preparation", so start preparing for your opportunity. Prepare with the end goal in mind. Equip yourself with the necessary tools to be successful. Visualize

65

yourself achieving success. In your preparation you will need to evaluate your situation, identify your strengths, weaknesses and gaps, research your competition, and create a strategic plan to carry out your goal.

Preparation accounts for about 70% of the four Ps. Abraham Lincoln said if you gave him six hours to chop down a tree that he would spend about 67% of that time sharpening the axe. Preparation reduces the possibilities of errors and stress and increases confidence and efficiency of your performance. Once you have completed your preparation, create a plan to practice.

Practice

The 2nd P is Practice. Practice allows you to "fall forward". Practice is about committing physically and mentally to repetition regularly. The more you practice the better your performance will be. There is a saying that practice makes perfect, but I think it is better said that prepared practice makes perfect practice. Prepared practice is effectively executing the plan you have drafted during the preparation stage and not just mindlessly going over drills.

Practice helps you develop skills that will increase your performance. Practice boosts your confidence and helps you be comfortable with being uncomfortable during your performance. Practice shows your growth, and when you are allowed to grow you can focus on the importance of persistence.

Persistence

Be persistent. No matter how difficult the task is, be persistent toward your goal. This can be the most frustrating stage of the four 4 Ps. Most people skip this stage because they do not want to go through the temporary pain.

This stage unfortunately forces many people to settle for mediocrity. This stage separates the good from the great. You have to go through the pain to get the reward. You have to be stubborn toward your goal. This stage is about being courageous enough to be successful. Being persistent is about striving to be better on every attempt.

To make it simple and break it down, if you have never shot a left-hand lay-up it will be difficult to make it, but the more you practice and be persistent the better you will be. Eventually, you are going to make that left-hand layup. If you have never lifted weights before it may be difficult to lift 150 pounds. Lifting 150 pounds may not come easy at first but with persistent practice you will be able to achieve your goal.

Persistence is about being focused and perfecting a skill. Bruce Lee said, "I fear not the man who has practiced 10,000 kicks once, but I fear the man who has practiced one kick 10,000 times." Persistence is where greatness lives. When you are persistent you are able to easily overcome adversity, barriers, and struggles. When you are ready to burst through that wall, then performance becomes natural.

Performance

Once you have prepared, practiced, and remained persistent, you are ready to rise to the occasion. This is the moment we live for, and because you are completely ready you will perform at your best. This stage should take only 5% to 7% of the total effort, due to work done in the other stages. Performance is all about executing and accomplishing your goal.

Take for example the Olympian Usain Bolt, or any pro athlete, who spent their entire life preparing and practicing for the Olympics. Usain stayed persistent to decrease his time over the years, and in 1996, he executed his goal by shattering the world record for 100-meter sprint at 9.58 seconds.

Think about that. Think about all of the years of preparation, the practicing, the frustration, the pain, the tears, the soreness, the injuries, the doubt, the persistence, the drive, the determination, the effort and the motivation it took for a performance of less than 10 seconds. That is mind-blowing, but that is greatness. That's how you get to your purpose, my friends.

Chapter 16

DEVELOP LEADERSHIP

Whether you believe leaders are born or made, it is possible for anyone to be a leader. Some leaders jump at the opportunity and others are either forced or stumble into leadership positions. However, I believe there are 5 qualities that can make you a great leader on your journey to find your purpose.

1. **Decision Making** – as a leader you are constantly making decisions. You are in that leadership position because someone trusts that you will make sound and rational decisions. As a leader, it is ok to make a wrong decision because you have an opportunity to grow and learn from it. But it should be unacceptable to not make a decision because you can put others at risk when you allow something to resolve itself.

2. **Problem Solving** – as long as you're a leader there will always be problems. You have to think of yourself as a firefighter. When there is a problem it is your responsibility to solve it.

3. **Adaptability** – leaders need to be flexible because in leadership nothing is always the same. You have to be ready for any situation that comes along and to produce great results from it.

4. **Accountability** – it is your responsibility as a leader to have integrity. You have to hold yourself and your team accountable for your responsibilities and what you all agree upon whenever you take a position.

5. **Motivational** – leaders need to have the ability to motivate others to action. Whether you inspire others by actions or by words, it is important to motivate your team to work towards a common goal.

If you focus on these 5 qualities, I am sure you will build confidence, enhance your skills, and become a great leader.

The Road Map

Do you have a roadmap to your purpose? When you are trying to find yourself or your purpose, take a road map or gps so you don't lose yourself. Remember there are no shortcuts to your purpose, but a roadmap will help you get there quicker. Your road map should include your life mission statement, personal vision statement, core values and board of directors.

Mission

Mission statements do not apply only to businesses. A personal mission statement gives you a reason for your existence, as well. Your life mission statement should be one to three sentences identifying what is important to you, who or what you want to serve, and what you expect to accomplish. Developing a mission statement brings clarity to your vision. It allows you to create goals and achieve them. Below is my personal mission statement.

My mission is to inspire and empower young people to overcome barriers for college and career readiness and success.

Now it is your turn. Research other examples of mission statements and write down a personal mission statement for life.

_____

_____

_____

_____

_____

_____

_____

_____

_____

_____

_____
_____
_____

Vision

A personal vision statement is a summary of the goals you want to accomplish. It communicates where you want to be in the future. To develop and fully understand your personal vision statement, you will need to travel back into your past and examine your personal experiences and analyze how these experiences have impacted or influence your life.

Identify how your outcomes or results have developed you into the person you are and the person you want to be. Your vision should be a sentence or a short paragraph communicating what is most important to you. After creating your personal vision statement explain why it is important to you. Below is my personal vision statement and why it is important to me.

My vision is to be a gateway for the youth to become successful adults.

Academically, for the most part of my life, I felt unprepared for college. College is truly like "A Different World" especially from where I come from.

As a first-generation college student, I felt lost and had a lack of guidance. I spent the majority of my life living in Charles Warner projects. I can admit the projects built me to be strong enough to survive college, but it definitely didn't prepare me academically and financially. Imagine a very curious and charismatic young man, away from home for the first time, with poor English, and street smarts trying to find his way on campus.

I admit I didn't go to college to learn. I went to college to be the first person in my entire family and among my friends to graduate from a four-year university. I was more motivated to change the narrative around my environment than to actually graduate to have a career. To be honest, I didn't really know I had to find a career until my senior year.

Throughout my college career, my grades were just good enough for me to not be expelled from college. I received similar grades in high school and junior college as well. My grades were a reflection of the poor choices I made to spend more time working my student job and hanging out late with friends rather than focus on studying. I can truly say that I enjoyed the social aspect of my college experience, which totally took a toll on my financial experience in college.

Coming from the projects, I never experienced many people, if any, receiving a lump sum of money every semester. As strange as this may sound, I felt like I was rich. However, I really don't believe that I got the memo about paying back my financial aid reward.

I wasn't ready for college but eventually I graduated. I became an educator and have spent my entire career developing and mentoring high school and college students. Over my professional career, I have been a student affair professional, an educator, an adjunct professor, a basketball coach, and mentor. I use my experiences as a student and professional to help give guidance and direction to engage students that may have or are having a similar college experience as mine.

There are so many of our students so unprepared for their college experience. Whether it is academically, financially, socially, or mentally, our students need guidance and direction to navigate them through their college experience. As college professionals, we are obligated to serve our students and ensure that they are prepared to succeed. College is truly a different world no matter where you come from, and I just hope I can help encourage, motivate, and inspire our students to make a better world wherever they come from.

Now it's your turn. Write your own personal vision statement here.

_____

_____

_____

_____

_____

_____

_____

_____

_____

_____

_____

_____

_____

_____

_____

_____

_____

_____

_____

_____

_____

_____

_____

Values

What are your core values? Do you stand for something? Malcolm X said, "if you don't stand for something, you will fall for anything." A great way to find out who you are and what you stand for is to develop your core values. Your core values stand on your foundation and support your purpose. Your core values are the things that are most important to you. Research a list of core values and identify 4-6 values that are most important to you and then define the values to help serve as a guide on your journey to your purpose.

Below is a list of my core values and a brief description of each value.

Service | Leadership | Openness | Accountability | Networking | Excellence

Service

"You will get all you want in life if you help enough other people get what they want," – Zig Ziglar.

We are all meant to serve in some capacity. Get involved and volunteer to help others that are in need of assistance. Volunteering gives you the opportunity to make new friends and build relationships, develop transferable and social skills, impact your well-being, and make you feel better as a person. To get involved and learn how you can volunteer, connect with your local community outreach. Make a difference in others' lives; you'll be glad you did.

Leadership

"The secret to success is good leadership, and good leadership is all about making the lives of your team members or workers better." – Tony Dungy.

Students should be engaged at their school. Join an organization, fraternity or sorority, group, club, or athletic team. It is important to grow your leadership by being a part of a group, organization, or team. You will develop many life and job skills to prepare you to become a better leader.

Openness

"Honesty and openness is always the foundation of insightful dialogue." – Bell Hooks

The beauty of the world is that you can meet many diverse people from different backgrounds, countries, or cultures. In meeting them, you may find that you have different beliefs and values, but you should take the time to explore and understand those differences and similarities. You will grow as a person with an open mind and learn new ideas and ways of the world.

Accountability

"At the end of the day we are accountable to our-selves – our success is a result of what we do." – Catherine Pulsifer.

It is on you and you alone to hold yourself ac-countable for your actions before you are re-sponsibility of holding others accountable.

Networking

"It's not what you know or who you know, but who knows you." – Susan RoAne.

Networking is one of the best tools to have in your toolbox. You can put yourself in better op-portunities with the relationships you build. Get outside of your comfort zone and find a mentor or job that is going to help position you for suc-cess. It is all about relationship building.

Excellence

"We are what we repeatedly do. Excellence, then, is not an act, but a habit." – Aristotle

Striving for excellence is key in life. Don't settle for anything less than your best work. As Les Brown says, "Shoot for the moon. Even if you miss, you'll land among the stars." I believe that excellence has more to do with effort than being smart.

Now that you have read my values, list your core values and define them to your life.

- _____
  _____
  _____
- _____
  _____
  _____
  _____
- _____
  _____
  _____
  _____
- _____
  _____
  _____
  _____
- _____
  _____
  _____
  _____
- _____
  _____
  _____
  _____

Personal Board of Directors

Having a personal board of directors is the next level to having mentors. Your BOD is responsible for mentoring, investing, advising, challenging, motivating and developing you to reach your full potential and purpose. Your Board should be readily available to you, a diverse group of people who are hopefully smarter than you, who can contribute differently than you, and who have your best interest at heart. Below, you can see the areas of my Personal Board of Directors. This group of people serve in a way that brings out the best in me. They develop me to reach my full potential daily.

> Areas of Personal Board of Directors
> Spiritual Development
> Leadership Development
> Professional Development
> Financial Development
> Social Development
> Communication Development
> Health & Wellbeing Development

Take a moment and think of some people in your life that will help you reach your full potential and your purpose. Write their names down and then ask them to serve on your personal BOD. You may not have many now, start to build those relationships with people that will be able to help get you to your purpose.

ETERNAL LIGHT

To shine your brightest light is
to be who you truly are."
- Roy T. Bennett

"Nothing can dim the light
that shines from within."
- Maya Angelou

"If you want to give light to others
you have to glow yourself."
– Thomas S. Monson

Chapter 17

YOU MATTER

One of the biggest questions you may ask yourself on your journey to your eternal light is "Why am I here?" or "What is my purpose?". We are all here for a reason. What you do matters. Your choices and decisions matter. Your life matters. You matter because you were born. You still matter because you are reading this book.

Do you know that you have greatness and excellence in you? I wrote a poem and part of the poem reads, "We are made of the earth, and just like the earth we have many precious stones and jewels buried deep inside of us; but we must search and dig deep within in order to find your fortune, your purpose."

I believe we have a responsibility to find our purpose because we are supposed to shine our light and inspire others to be great. If my mom, the boys and girls club, Chris McGee, or Dr. Dennis Kimbro didn't inspire me, I may not be writing this book right now to inspire you. If there wasn't a Michael Jordan would we have a Lebron James?

If there wasn't an Oprah Winfrey would we have an Ellen DeGeneres? If there wasn't a Martin Luther King Jr. would we have a President Barack Obama? The world would be less bright without them. So, ask yourself who is waiting on you to inspire them. Who is waiting for you to turn on your light? What you do matters. Your purpose matters. You have a responsibility to find your purpose.

Chapter 18

THE FINAL GLOW

We all have our talents and abilities that make certain things slightly easier for us than others. Whether it is being able to play sports, being able to cook, or being able to lead people, some talents and abilities seem to come naturally. However, not just some of us, but all of us have a gift inside of us given by God.

This gift is our purpose, the reason why we are here. A lot of people are searching for their gifts externally, but God has placed our gift in the safest place where no one has access to it but you. You have to work hard and search deep down inside of yourself to find it. When you find it, you will know it because it is like the final level or the "glow" in the movie The Last Dragon!

The Last Dragon is one of my favorite movies. It is a martial arts comedy film produced by Berry Gordy in 1985. It is about a martial artist named Leroy Green, also known as Bruce Leroy, in search of the final level, the "glow". The movie starts with Leroy's teacher informing him that there is nothing else he can teach him, and that he would have to find the final level on his own.

Leroy then goes on a wild goose chase to find a master to give him something he already possesses. Leroy searched all around the city only to find out that this master he searches for doesn't exist. He returned to his teacher and asked, "why have you sent me on a journey to find someone who does not exist?" His teacher responded with one of my favorite lines in the movie. Handing a fortune cookie to Leroy, he says, "Here, it contains everything you need to find your way to the golden glow." Leroy opens the cookie and finds it empty. "Think Leroy! You have just opened a fortune cookie without a fortune, written by a master who does not exist, to find a solution to a problem whose answer you already know." And then he added, "There is one place that you have not looked, and it is there, only there that you shall find the master". In the movie, Leroy encountered many obstacles, a romantic love story, and the ultimate fight with his archrival, Sho Nuff. During the epic fight with Sho Nuff, Bruce Leroy realizes that he had the "glow" inside of him the entire time. Bruce Leroy defeats his archrival, wins the girl, and finally discovers his true self.

A lot of us are just like Bruce Leroy, we are ready to experience the final level, the "glow", our gift, but we are too busy searching in all of the wrong places. Many of us are looking for confirmation or permission to be great, but God has already given us that permission when he placed the "glow" inside of us. So, use your energy to look deep inside yourself for the ultimate "glow", and when you find your gift, use it to light up the world!

THE GREATEST INSPIRATION

There is a power within you
An inner strength you will find
In time of struggle
In time of need
It is the mystery of life
Where you become one
With your mind, body and soul
And Truth be told
It is that ever elusive glow
That only you can hold

You are a master
A master of your own mind
Designed in His image
A master without limits

You are a master
A master redefined
By a power that is given
From a Master without limits
Do you believe?
Do you believe
That there is a fire burning internally

A gift given to you at birth
Waiting to be unlocked
An eternal light
That leads you to your purpose
Will you search for it?
Will you fight for it?
Will you sacrifice your life for it?
It is yours to have
To share
To hold
To own
You have the key to your destiny
Don't just stand at the door of serenity
Open it
Walk through it
Embrace it
Live it
Give your life to it
And it will be given to you
The power of understanding, wisdom
and courage
You deserve it
But you must believe
In order to receive
A gift from a Master
Created for a master
To inspire other masters
Is the final glow
And when you reached your destination
You will know
It is the greatest inspiration

APPENDIX

Questionnaire 1

• Have you ever felt like you were not good enough? If so, what was the situation?

    • Truth be told, there are too many times where I don't feel that I am good enough. I find that I question myself and my abilities all the time. For various reasons I am battling fear of rejection, success, or even stagnation. I will use my recent novel as an example. The process of writing it was difficult because I had doubts on whether I could finish it and when I did then I feared that no one would read it, and those that did wouldn't like it. Now, I battle with myself when it comes to looking at numbers. How many books did I sell today? Have people rated it and reviewed it? When those things fall through or the numbers are low, those thoughts creep back to me. Am I not good enough?

    It can be a constant struggle of fear and courage. I understand that fear is paralyzing, and it is because of that I strive to move past it.

- In that situation, how did you respond to your feelings?
  - When the feelings get bad or close to overwhelming, I ask myself, "what am I afraid of?" I tend to mentally jot down things that I might be feeling. Am I scared that I put myself out there too much? Maybe I am scared that I am not ready for the attention or perhaps I am ultimately afraid of failure. All these feed into this mindset that perhaps I am not good enough to be a writer. I'm taking a leap of faith and I am not sure where I am going to land.

    My point is that I try very hard to listen to myself. The reason I am a writer is that I am able to put my emotions on paper and it makes me feel so much better. My blog has been a place where I can release pent up feelings and emotions. The reality is that I am good enough. I just need to convince myself on occasion of this fact. Even answering these questions in written form is making me feel better about myself.

- What were the results?
  - The results are simple. I continue to follow the path I set for myself. I cannot and will not stop until I am satisfied with where my life is. I decided to go on this path of being an author and I know that is something no one can take away from me.

- What would be your best advice to someone who is feeling as if they were not good enough?
  - My advice is this, no one ever feels good enough. Did that stop the most successful people from being what they became? Not at all. Not feeling good enough is a product of fear that we create in our minds. Once we get out of our own way, we will feel good enough.

- What do you think are some of the reasons people may feel as if they are not good enough?
  - I mention fear a lot because I think that it is a universal trait that can paralyze us. I also think about lack of self-worth which leads into not believing in ourselves. Who is going to love us or believe in us (besides family) if we do not believe in and

93

love ourselves? It sounds simple but it really isn't. Fear and low self-value make it hard to set goals and accomplish life's dreams. Once I was finally fed up with my own personal struggles, I set some goals for myself and decided to make those goals a reality.

- Has someone ever told you that you weren't good enough?
  - No one has told me directly that I wasn't good enough, however, there have been many actions that other people do in which this feeling can come out. Whether it is my high school guidance counselor telling me that I would never get accepted to Syracuse University or a professor intentionally giving me a low grade, these things affected me. It made me want to prove people wrong and I feel like I have been doing that my whole life.

- Did you believe them? Why or why not?
  - In those instances above, I didn't believe them. I didn't believe them because I knew I was better than my grades and my behavior, I

wanted to prove to them that I am as smart and as capable as anyone else, but my biggest opponent has always been me.

- What would a person need to feel as if they were good enough?
  - Everyone needs a support system. This goes beyond relationships and love. Yes, love will help you get through the day but a genuine support system of people pushing you to be better is what we all need. I'm not sure where I would be right now if I did not have people telling me I can be an author.

- What area(s) in your life do you feel (or have you felt) as if you are not good enough?
  - It has always been in my creative side and my love life that I felt I was not good enough. I've never felt this way about my job though. Work is the only place where I can say without blinking that I am good at this. However, when it comes to love and life, it can be a mess. It all comes down to self-worth. As a teenager I never thought I was good enough

to go out there and get a girlfriend. I was terrified of girls. At the same time, I never thought I was good enough to a writer. But now, in my 40's, I have the courage to publish something.

- If you were to describe how it felt to not be good enough what words would you use?

  - I'm an emotional person so feeling not enough is horrible. There is sadness, fear, and general unhappiness that can lead to anger (and that was when I was younger). Now, it is more of a nagging feeling in my gut, a nervousness that sometimes won't go away unless I address it.

- If you were to describe how it felt to not be good enough what words would you use?

  - It depends on the day. My friends and my wife often remind me that I am indeed good enough and that I overthink everything. Sometimes family will make me feel better as well. You can never underestimate the power of love and family. I also use other people as motivation. I see people doing their thing and I realize that I can do what I want as well.

I also want to mention that feeling supported in my endeavors makes me feel that I am doing the right things. Some people will talk about supporting you but not put their words into action. Others, from whom you would never expect it provide exactly the support you need. I'm not talking about just money. Every bit as important are words of encouragement and belief in someone. For me it was trusting someone enough to share with them things that I had written. Support is very important, which is why I did this interview. I need to support those who support me.

Questionnaire 2

* Have you ever felt like you were not good enough?
    * There are have been plenty of times in my life where I have felt that I am not good enough. I believe that that is a daily struggle for many. There are still times when I question myself and my ability to do well at my job and as a parent.

- If so, what was the situation?
  - If I were to pick one situation it would be the day that I was hired at the Gifford Foundation. Prior to being hired at the foundation I worked for a local nonprofit for almost six years. I knew I wanted more for myself. I felt that I had plateaued in that particular position and I knew they would not offer me a management position. When I was hired at the foundation I was extremely enthusiastic but scared of the unknown and constantly questioning myself: why they hired me in the first place, why did they feel that my opinion mattered, who was I to provide them with advice on who should and should not get funding. It was almost like staring in a role that I never auditioned for, with no formal training, and figuring out things as I went.

- In that situation, how did you respond to your feelings?
  - I responded to my feelings by always looking for validation that demonstrated that I was doing a good job. I asked a lot of questions,

studied how other co-workers did
their jobs and imitated their actions.

- What were the results?
  - These feelings caused me to sec-
    ond guess myself, questioning all of
    my decisions and not speaking up
    during meetings. The result was my
    getting lost in the crowd and my
    perspective and opinion not being
    shared. It eroded my value as an
    asset to the organization, and de-
    creased what I brought to the table
    as a team member and a staff per-
    son.

- What would be your best advice to someone who is feeling as if they were not
  good enough?
  - My advice would be to surround
    yourself with positive messages
    and positive people. I started put-
    ting positive quotes on my desk
    and I also was fortunate enough to
    have a mentor who helped me think
    through the reasons why I felt not
    good enough. One of the reasons
    I discovered was my own self-con-
    sciousness about my credentials. I
    felt that people were judging me

because I did not have a bachelor's degree, when in reality I was judging myself. So, I decided to go back to school and get a bachelor's degree. Without the encouragement of my mentor, I am not sure if I ever would have taken that leap of faith to further my education. I also wrote my own personal mission, which I keep in clear view for me to see. The quotes that I keep around are: "Trust your crazy ideas" – Dan Zadra and "What lies behind us and what lies before us are small matters compared to what lies within us" – Ralph Waldo Emerson. These are just a few methods that not only help me stay positive but also give me the courage to believe that I am good enough and I deserve the blessings that I have received.

- What do you think are some of the reasons people may feel as if they are not good enough?
  - There are many reasons why someone may not feel good enough. It could be because they've been told that they are not good enough so often that they begin to believe it.

It could be due to intimidation from others or the fear of failure. However, no matter what the reason is, it most likely comes from within. Self-doubt and fear are two of the largest barriers for someone trying to move forward but not really sure how to get to their destiny. This is why having a supportive mentor is imperative.

- What do you think are some of the reasons people may feel as if they are not good enough?
  - No one has ever said to my face, "you are not good enough". However, many times actions speak louder than words. I have experienced management implying that I didn't have the capacity or skill set needed to be promoted within the organization. I have had family give up on me due to decisions I made earlier in life. I have been overlooked for work that I have done, and others have taken credit for it. Those are all signs and actions demonstrating that I am not good enough.

- Did you believe them? Why or why not?

- There were times when I did believe those who said was not good enough and just accept it. However, I started to realize that accepting it caused me to limit myself. There is a saying that "you don't know what you don't know" and I didn't know that not everyone had my best interest in mind. I just believed what people told me. I drank the Kool-Aid without asking any questions or making any improvements for my own personal growth.

- What would a person need to feel as if they were good enough?
    - I believe that a person needs several things in order to feel like they are good enough. That person needs to have confidence, they need to be competent, and they need to believe that they are capable and able to handle the task at hand. Some people just need a chance, an opportunity, someone to believe in them and show them that they have potential. Others just need to hear someone say, "you're good enough" or "you deserve this" or "you can do it". Still others just want to be

heard. As a society we talk but we don't do a good job at listening. Everyone has a story to tell and they just want to be heard.

- What area(s) in your life do you feel (or have felt) as if you are not good enough?
  - My career path has had its challenges. I work in an environment where I don't see many people who look like me. I work in an environment that is controlled mostly by white men, which can be extremely intimidating. These types of situations cause even the most confident person to question themselves. I continue to question why I have been invited to certain meetings or to be a part of specific projects. There are times that I feel like the token minority at the table. This continues to be a struggle for me. But I don't believe that it is a bad thing to question yourself at times. This causes me to really think about what I want to say and helps me articulate things better. Being invited to decision-making tables also puts me in a position to figure how I can incorporate inviting others and

suggesting that organizations be more inclusive. I have taken the energy created by fear and doubt and redirected it to create change. I still wonder if I am good enough, but I think it is healthy to reassess yourself from time to time. The other area in my life that continues to be a lifetime struggle is parenting. I think every parent questions whether they are good enough for this job. It is a struggle to not blame yourself for decisions that your children make or how they turn out as adults. There are plenty of books out there that claim they have the answers, but they don't. Parenting is hard, period. However, it is important to have in the decisions that you make and be willing to listen and learn from your mistakes.

- If you were to describe how it felt to not be good enough what words would you use?
    - The words that come to mind are degrading, depressing, unappreciated, defeated and at a loss for words. I was disappointed in myself for not being good enough, angry

at the person for judging or making the assumption that I was not good enough and fearful of not ever being good enough.

- When you felt this way who or what motivated you to feel otherwise?
  - Having faith in a higher power has always kept me going, but I would be remiss if I didn't mention my mother, who has been a true supporter in everything that I have done in life. She motivates me and I have learned from her personal mistakes. Becoming a mother has motivated me to be push forward so that I can be an example and role model for my children. I do my best to surround myself with positive people who continue to encourage me to be better and do better. Then there are the times that I have to convince myself that everything is going to be okay. People can encourage and motivate me all day, but at the end of the day I have to believe it and be willing to do what is necessary to achieve it.

Questionnaire 3

- Have you ever felt like you were not good enough? In that situation, how did you respond to your feelings? What were the results?

  - Yes, but not often. I played basketball and volleyball in high school, and I was a captain of both teams. Holding a leadership role is both a privilege and a burden, as the joys and struggles of the endeavor are magnified. I remember one basketball game in particular, my senior year of high school. It was a home game against one of our rival teams, and I had an absolutely terrible game. I felt defeated and didn't know how to deal with it at first. I cried for a long, long time after the game. I had a great number of supporters, including my coach and my parents, who were there for me. However, this was a situation that I needed to deal with myself. During the game, I had tried to do too many things, and I lost myself as a player somewhere along the way. After the initial frustration of the game, I was able to take a step back from the situation. I knew that

I couldn't change what happened, I could only control how I responded to it. I spoke with my teammates, explaining the way I felt, and told them how I was going to work to improve both my individual play and our team play. While we still hit some roadblocks as a team, I saw an improvement in my individual play. I still had the same skill level, but I made an effort to increase my confidence.

- What would be your best advice to someone who is feeling as if they are not good enough?
  - Talk it out! Speaking from experience, it does wonders to talk about your problems. That's why it's so important to maintain relationships with people who are supportive, understanding, and great at listening. I credit my sanity to my family and friends, because they're always there to listen to me. I would also suggest positive self-talk. It sounds odd at first, I know. But to be able to tell yourself that YOU are good enough, and to believe it, is something that will truly change your life.

107

- What do you think are some of the reasons people may feel as though they are not good enough?
  - Bad experiences are inevitable. We all have our bad days, and we all make mistakes. Sometimes, a bad day can really lower your self-esteem. We all go through times when we feel like we aren't good enough, but we need to realize that we're not alone in feeling this way.

- Has someone ever told you that you weren't good enough?
  - No, and if they did, I would do my best to move on from any relationship I had with them. I take pride in the fact that I surround myself with positive people who make ME a better person. Negativity is a waste of my time.

- What would a person need to feel as if they were good enough?
  - Sometimes a nod of support is all you need. A smile and a little praise go a long way, so remember to smile, beautiful people!

- In what area(s) in your life do you feel as

though you are not good enough?

-     I'm not perfect in any sense of the word. But I truly believe that I'm good enough to do whatever I want, whatever I work for in my life. There might always be someone who's better than I am, but there's no one who will ever be me.

- If you were to describe how it felt to not be good enough, what words would you use?
  -     For lack of a better way to put it, it sucks. People can be mean, and sometimes we are even mean to ourselves. But I really try hard to avoid people and situations that make me feel low about myself, because I know I'm worth more than that.

- When you felt this way, who or what motivated you to feel otherwise?
  -     My family, friends, and mentors are my biggest support systems, and often they're my biggest motivators. However, nothing can take the place of self-motivation. Someone could be handed a million dollars to fulfill their dream, but if they weren't

self-motivated to put in any effort, their money, and dream, would be wasted.

Questionnaire 4

- Have you ever felt like you were not good enough? If so, what was the situation?
    - I lost my hearing completely when I was 20 years old. It was the summer before second year at university - When I had finished my freshman year, I could hear; when I returned in September, I was completely deaf. I really struggled with what being disabled would mean for who I was. I was treated as a completely differ-ent person than I had experienced as a hearing person. I had always been outgoing and social and now I felt trapped inside my own body.

- In that situation, how did you respond to your feelings?
    - I felt so many things at that time. I suppose some were feelings of inadequacy. But I was also over-whelmed with problems related to my hearing loss. I remember my mom saying that everyone would understand if I wanted to quit

school or take time off to adjust. The thought hadn't yet crossed my mind. While I hadn't considered school or my friends or any future whatsoever, I panicked at the idea of changing anything in my life because of what I was experiencing.

- What were the results?
  - I returned to school in the fall. It wasn't a courageous decision – although sticking by it required courage. I knew there would come a time in my life when the deafness wasn't new, and I had come to terms with it. I didn't want to lose time and withdraw from my life and goals because I felt blindsided at the moment. Time was going to pass regardless, and I wasn't going to become who I wanted to be by skipping life experiences like my first house with friends and the college experience as a whole.

  - The most difficult part of going back was seeing everyone I had met and known the year before. There was an element of embarrassment in explaining what had happened.

Even worse was meeting new people for the first time because they only knew me as deaf. My twin sister moved in with me (and my roommates) for the first month of school. She was with me everywhere I went and made things much easier just by the way she approached my new disability – it wasn't something I became, but rather something that happened to me and I was still Chrissie. I feel like she was strong and confident for me and I sort of followed her lead until I felt that way myself. I graduated from college on time with my friends and went on the following year to law school where I graduated in 2009.

- What would be your best advice to someone who is feeling as if they were not good enough?
  - The best advice I can give is to lie to yourself when you believe the truth is that you're not good enough. It's amazing how easy it is to believe whatever you choose. It's easy to convince yourself that you can't do something because you're not smart enough, or good looking enough, or

hard working enough or the million other reasons we give ourselves to justify not doing something. Being deaf is just another one of these silly excuses I could give myself. Instead, I prefer to work around it. I'm always conscious that I miss out on a lot because I can't hear, but not in a way that makes me feel sorry for myself. I always try to remember I've got to work twice as hard to do half as well. Another lie I tell myself to keep at the grind.

- What do you think are some of the reasons people may feel as if they are not good enough?
  - I think people assume others have it all figured out and that they themselves don't. That they're missing qualities people must possess to achieve certain things. I barely graduated high school because I was a goof and just couldn't be bothered going to class. Then I graduated and realized I didn't know anything! I went to community college for one year and then joined my friends for the first year in university. I worked my butt off

to get into university and I remember when I got there thinking, 'well these people aren't that special. They're just like me.' Then I worked very hard to get into law school and I went to the top school in Canada. I thought I wouldn't fit in and that I wasn't smart enough to be there. Much to my disappointment, my classmates were just people like me. The experience taught me that people who do things that are "special" are just people who have taken the right steps and worked hard at small things for a long time to get to where they are. This experience gave me the courage to try my lifetime goal to be a comic, which I was sure had become impossible when I lost my hearing.

- Being deaf has become something I have had to deal with regardless of what I'm doing. I'd much prefer to be a deaf comic than a deaf lawyer! Regardless of what I choose to do, I will be a deaf-something. So, I've learned not to let being deaf keep me from pursuing anything I want in life.

- I stepped on a comedy stage for the first time when I was 28. I had worried for years that I wouldn't be good enough because I was deaf; but being on stage, the only thing that worries me, is whether I'm funny enough. I believe I am. But that alone is never enough. Talent only takes anyone so far. If I can work hard enough, I'm positive I can be good enough to do anything. That doesn't mean I can become an expert in anything, but good enough only means doing what it takes to do something. It certainly includes working around your disadvantages in order to be who you want to be.

Questionnaire 5

- Have you ever felt like you were not good enough? If so, what was the situation?
  - Unfortunately, I struggled with several areas in my life of feeling like I was not good enough: Academics, athletics, healthy eating habits, relationships, friendships, my outward appearance, and even in my worthiness to be a Christian. In these situations, I usually felt like I was not good enough because I was trying

to please other people, not actually because I personally wanted to grow in this area or felt I was incapable of excelling.

- In that situation, how did you respond to your feelings?
    - In each situation, I always thought I was average. I felt as if I always needed to push harder to prove I could be good enough in each of these areas. Or the converse, I would settle for average because I allowed negativity to consume me and make me believe that I could not do any better.

- What were the results?
    - The results of believing that I was not good enough led to a few different results. One result led to bitterness towards the person who made me feel that way. Another result would be the desire to change my behavior and attitude about the areas where I did not feel good enough, as long as it did not conflict with my morals.

- What would be your best advice to some-one who is feeling as if they were not good enough?
  - Repetition of positive affirmations can be a very positive tool to help someone grow in this area. When I struggled with low self-esteem, for example, I would look in the mir-ror every night and tell myself that "I was beautiful", until I believed it myself.

- What do you think are some of the rea-sons people may feel as if they are not good enough?
  - Just like me, I believe people may feel like they are not good enough because they compare themselves to others or try to live to the stan-dards that other people place on them.

- Has someone ever told you that you weren't good enough?
  - I cannot remember a time where someone specifically told me that I was not good enough, but their ac-tions spoke louder than words.

- Did you believe them? Why or why not?
  - I did believe that I was not good enough because I was not consistently uplifted from my direct family that I was.

- What would a person need to feel as if they were good enough?
  - I believe many of our insecurities originate from childhood experiences. If children are raised to believe that they are good enough, then that will carry over into their adulthood.

- If you were to describe how it felt to not be good enough what words would you use?
  - Worthless. Unwanted. Unworthy. Average/Mediocre. Unmotivated.

- When you felt this way who or what motivated you to feel otherwise?
  - When I felt like I was not good enough, my uncles, my godmother, some of my best friends, poets in the P4CM (Passion For Christ Movement), motivational speakers, Christian rap artists, and reading the Bible helped me fight my doubts and the lies of being not good enough.

Questionnaire 6

- Have you ever felt like you were not good enough? If so, what was the situation?
  - In early college, I was talking with the mother of a High School friend and telling her my plans for the years ahead. I wanted to pursue multiple disciplines of engineering, and then incorporate them into a combination of practice and research. "Wow," she said, "that's very...ambitious!" The implication being, that's crazy and you won't be able to do that. For better or worse, I was not accustomed to negative feedback growing up, so it took me a while to register what she was saying. It hurt.

  - Another example was not an interpersonal interaction, but a situation in which I'd placed myself. After two years in a middle-tier state school, I decided to pursue a degree at my childhood dream Ivy League school. I was able to transfer. When I got there, it was everything I'd expected - stimulating, inspiring and academically rigorous. On top of this were many of the world's wealthiest and smartest people. I was intimidated to say the least.

- In that situation, how did you respond to your feelings?
  - My emotional response to "Mrs. Reality's" assessment of my goals went through a range. I was first offended, then angered, then self-doubtful and finally circumspect. The fact of the matter was that my bravado had gotten the best of me. Of course, that plan was ridiculous. There was a very small possibility that I would have been able to accomplish it, but at what cost? From the expense of such an academic endeavor to the excessive time and effort spent, it was excessive to think I should gain mastery of so many disciplines. Any one of them gives a lifetime of work and opportunities for improvement and achievement. Really, what I needed to do, I came to understand, was to pick one general direction and pursue it, enthusiastically and expeditiously.

  - I buckled down, kept off the recreation, worked my butt off, and did well. Even in the summer before entering school, I took a couple of community college classes, and worked out intensely to be at the top of my game in the fall.

- What were the results?
  - For the first, I adjusted my expectations. I thoughtfully considered the "negative feedback" and assessed its validity. Sometimes there are simply things that we are "not good enough for", not because we are weak or unable, but because they exceed the bounds of reasonableness. I am also "not good enough" to swim across the Atlantic, no matter how dedicated to that dream I may be.

  - For the second, I worked hard and did well, and was awarded a fellowship to pursue a master's degree in my field.

- What would be your best advice to someone who is feeling as if they were not good enough?

- You can probably do it, but in addition to your drive and determination, your plan and approach also need to be fully thought through. Determine the timeline of your goal: is it a six-month plan to lose 60 lbs., a four-year plan to get a degree, an open-ended timeline to do something like build your own house? Knowing the scale of your goal will help you adjust your expectations regarding measurement of success.

- What do you think are some of the reasons people may feel as if they are not good enough?
  - Life is hard. Avoiding challenge and putting in the bare minimum can be a course of action that gets you through life. Going beyond that is scary and has obstacles. People around you who are just coasting through life will also be jealous haters, ready to put you down.

- What would a person need to feel as if they were good enough?
  - A person with a large and seemingly insurmountable goal can feel overwhelmed. What they need is a plan

with milestones, so that they can have achievements along the way to build confidence and power them to the next challenge. Organization and planning. Checklists. Preparatory notes, reflective notes. Keep a journal of where you are and where you're headed and your thoughts and feelings along the way. This can be both a guideline along the way and could be a proud document of reflection later in life.

- What area(s) in your life do you feel (or have felt) as if you are not good enough?
  - Pretty much any that are worth doing. It is what makes me want to work on them.

- If you were to describe how it felt to not be good enough what words would you use?
  - Depressing and discouraging to the point where it can affect my performance in other areas, even those in which I usually feel I'm plenty good.

- When you felt this way who or what motivated you to feel otherwise?

- Right now, I'm working on a large project with a fair amount of risk that requires a lot of input from me. I have been mostly following the advice I set out above, but sometimes, I'm not motivated - I don't care to be pursuing it. But the thing is the long game. I am motivated because the ultimate goal is more than 1.5 years in the future, but I have a set of milestones - and a to-do list - for the next two weeks. I only need to get those done for now and use smaller victories to keep me feeling like I can do this.

- If you're feeling like you're not good enough for something, that means that you're thinking about it, and you want to be good enough to do it. That alone counts for a lot but is only part one of the journey. Persistence and organization are the second part.

Questionnaire 7

- Have you ever felt like you were not good enough? If so, what was the situation?

- For example, I felt like I wasn't good enough as a musician in a jam session where others were more confident, more knowledgeable, better prepared, and who were judgmental.

- In that situation, how did you respond to your feelings?

  - I would have a drink or two to calm my nerves and try to have fun with it. Sometimes I wouldn't play at all or just play a really short solo and get off stage. Sometimes I would try to overcompensate and be super confident and strong on the outside but would feel incredibly insecure on the inside. Sometimes I would drink too much and sound even worse than I would with all those nerves, and then really regret playing at all. I would make a mental note to learn and practice whatever I didn't know and write down notes and just stay and listen.

- What were the results?

  - The problem was that it was sometimes too overwhelming, and I just didn't practice or do anything about it and ended up in the same situation again by being uncomfortable at jam sessions. Or whatever I needed to work on really just didn't inspire me enough for me to actually want to learn it at home. Sometimes I would mull over it forever and ask questions like, did I get applause and compliments because I am a woman and that is rare for people to see? Or did they not like me or take me seriously for that same reason? Did he get my number because he actually likes my playing and would want to work with me or is he just trying to get a date? Did I never get asked to be in that band because the band is all black people and I am white? I would open up conversations about stuff like that, but many others were not interested, especially since most of my peers were black men and I was the outsider in that situation.

- What would be your best advice to someone who is feeling as if they were not good enough?

- It depends on the situation. If someone told someone they are not good enough, I would say that the person who said that probably has their own problems that they are dealing with and they are trying to push it onto someone else. If they are just not confident enough, I would try to compliment them, and encourage them. My mantra is just to stay positive, focus on the things you can do, not the things you can't, and just take it one step at a time.

- What do you think are some of the reasons people may feel as if they are not good enough?

  - Lack of self-confidence often comes from outside influences telling you that you should be something you are not. The media has a lot to do with body image issues, with a specific image of what is sexy and attractive - mostly unattainable ideas. When women dress and act like what is accepted as sexy, they are labeled as slutty in real-life and are wanted, but not respected. There are so many double standards

127

out there and I feel like the journey to finding yourself and being confident from within is a pretty rough road, especially for young women in terms of physical appearance.

- Did you believe them? Why or why not?

  - Yes and no. It never really bounced off without affecting me in some way, even if I didn't believe them.

- What would a person need to feel as if they were good enough?

  - They would have to feel it from within, and not expect it to come from anyone else on the outside.

- What area(s) in your life do you feel (or have felt) as if you are not good enough?

  - As a musician, in my career, in social settings, and in terms of physical attractiveness and relationships

- If you were to describe how it felt to not be good enough what words would you use?

- • Anxious, embarrassed, depressed, hurt.
- • When you felt this way who or what motivated you to feel otherwise?

  - • Reassurance from friends and family, venting with other people who have gone through similar situations, going to the gym, being proactive in a positive way to battle my insecurities one step at a time.

About the Author

Seneca Wilson is a motivational speaker committed to serving as a gateway for young people to become successful adults. He is on a mission to inspire and empower young people to overcome barriers for college and career readiness and success. Through service, leadership, openness, accountability, networking, and excellence, Seneca is able to connect, engage, and impact young people. Today, many students are graduating from high school unprepared for the next level. Seneca wants to empower young people to increase graduation rates and college enrollment rates while helping decrease school dropout rates and unemployment rates.

WWW.SENECAWILSON.COM

Made in the USA
Columbia, SC
06 November 2020